Snap books™

Cheerleading

Cheer Essentials

Uniforms and Equipment

by Jen Jones

Capstone press

Mankato, Minnesota

Snap Books are published by Capstone Press,
151 Good Counsel Drive, P.O. Box 669, Mankato, Minnesota 56002
www.capstonepress.com

Library of Congress Cataloging-in-Publication Data
Jones, Jen, 1976-
  Cheer essentials: uniforms and equipment / by Jen Jones.
      p. cm. — (Snap books cheerleading)
  Includes index.
  ISBN 0-7368-4360-4 (hardcover)
  1. Cheerleading — Equipment and supplies — Juvenile literature.
  2. Cheerleaders — Uniforms — Juvenile literature. I. Title. II. Series.
  LB3635.J655 2006
  791.6'4'0284 — dc22   2005007270

Summary: A guide for children and pre-teens on uniforms and equipment
for cheerleading.

Editor: Deb Berry/Bill SMITH STUDIO
Illustrators: Lisa Parett; Roxanne Daner, Marina Terletsky and Brock Waldron/Bill SMITH STUDIO
Designers: Marina Terletsky, and Brock Waldron/Bill SMITH STUDIO
Photo Researcher: Iris Wong/Bill SMITH STUDIO

Photo Credits: Cover: Getty Images; 6, Hulton Archive/Getty Images; 8-10, Dennis MacDonald/Alamy;
12, PhotoDisc Red/Getty Images; 14, PhotoDisc Green/Getty Images; 17, Wayrynen/NewSport/Corbis;
20, Bob Daemmrich/The Image Works; 28, PhotoDisc; 32, Britton Lenahan. Back Cover, Getty Images.
All other photos by Tim Jackson Photography.

1 2 3 4 5 6 10 09 08 07 06 05

Table of Contents

Must Have Cheer Essentials

Picture the gym floor right before a big competition. It's a sea of school colors, skirts, and smiles. How can you stand out from the other squads? Having your own special team style makes a big difference. It's the first thing the judges and crowd notice when your team steps out on the floor. Looking your best is key to performing your best.

4

Attractive uniforms, poms, and eye-catching **accessories** all make up your team's look. Cheer essentials like these are an important need for the school and the squad. Many of these materials are used year after year, so you should always take good care of them. The next owner will thank you when it's time to pass down the poms.

This book shows you the hottest cheer styles and most useful essentials. We also give you great money-making ideas to help your squad snag the latest and greatest items.

Get ready to suit up and step out in style!

"Looking your best is key to performing your best!"

You've Got the Look

From the long, flowing skirts of the 1950s to the short, bouncy skirts of today, cheer fashion has come a long way. Let's take a look at how cheer fashion has changed over the years.

In the old days, female cheerleaders wore very long, heavy skirts because girls were expected to "cover up" back then. They also wore button-down blouses and letter sweaters for a clean-cut image. Black-and-white saddle shoes were all the rage, too.

REMEMBER!

As cheerleading has become more of a real sport, skirt lengths have risen above the knee to allow for more movement. Snug-fitting, sleek **shell tops** have replaced all those big sweaters of the past. Comfortable **crosstrainers** are now a must for meeting the athletic demands of the sport.

Body types, quality, comfort, and how much you can spend are all important things to consider when choosing uniforms. You're representing your school, so it's a must that you behave with class and wear tasteful uniforms that make you look your best. Follow these rules, and you're sure to be dressed for success.

Seasons Change

Just like the mail, cheerleaders show up come rain, sleet, or snow. Unless the weather is so bad that the sports team can't compete, you're expected to be there on the sidelines. (Smiling and cheering, of course!)

Luckily, cheerleaders for indoor sports get to stay warm in the heat of the gym. Football cheerleaders don't have that luck, so it's important to remember that when choosing uniforms. Try on these weather-wise tips for size.

34

Shiver in Style For football, consider a long-sleeved, turtleneck sweater with matching skirt. Cheer jackets and leggings can also be worn, along with winter clothing in school colors. Just make sure you can still move easily after all that bundling.

What's "In" for Indoors Indoor cheerleaders have more freedom when choosing cheer gear. Halters and sleeveless shells are very popular in tops. Straight skirts with clean lines have replaced the heavy, pleated skirts of the past.

 "Wow" Warm-Ups

Want to spread the cheer spirit on and off the sidelines? Do it with team warm-up suits. Warm-ups are usually worn before games and competitions. You can also sport them to school on game days to show your squad pride.

" Do it with team warm-up suits! "

Warm-up suits are two-piece sets in cotton or nylon. They are made up of a zip-up jacket or V-neck jersey and comfortable pants. Set yours apart from other teams by adding your name or team **logo**.

Why buy a warm-up? First of all, they add something exciting to the usual cheer uniform. They cut down on uniform wear and tear because they can be worn instead of a team outfit. Wearing a warm-up also prevents your uniform from getting dirty while you stretch and practice.

Although it's a good idea to get warm-up suits, they can be an expensive addition to all the other equipment that a team must buy. For some fabulous **fund-raiser** ideas, check out pages 28 and 29.

Fancy Footwork

All that cheering and dancing can really give your feet a workout. Choosing the right shoes can protect your feet. Many shoe companies make special cheer shoes to make stunting easier. When choosing your shoes, consider these factors.

Comfort Are the shoes big and heavy or lightweight? Do the shoes have enough padding and support?

Price and Quality The average cheerleading shoes cost about $50 to $60. Do the shoes you want fall within your price range? Are they sturdy enough to last the whole year or longer?

Purpose What is your squad's purpose? Athletic squads should buy **shock absorbent shoes**. Dance teams should buy lightweight crosstrainers.

Look Do you want simple white shoes or shoes with fancy designs and logos? How many colors do you want to include?

Do some research before buying your shoes. Have your coach or parents read magazines, books, or websites that do product surveys. This research might help you learn if other people who bought the shoes were happy with them. If the survey company has tested the shoes, they might tell you how sturdy they are and how likely they are to hurt your feet.

"Choosing the right shoes can protect your feet."

Chapter 2

Pom Power

Since the 1930s, cheerleaders have used pom-poms to accent their routines. The first poms were made of paper, but in 1965, inventor Fred Gastoff introduced the vinyl poms we know today. Three cheers for Fred!

The sky's the limit when choosing between different styles and shapes. Though most teams go for poms in their school colors, decisions must be made on the length, width, and look of the **strands**. Metallic, glitter, and two-toned strands are just a few of the popular styles available. The most popular handle is the "show baton," which is hidden inside the pom.

When your poms arrive, you might be surprised at the way they look. They won't look like the poms you saw in the catalog! It's your job to fluff your new poms before use.

How to fluff your new pom-poms

Separate the strands if they are in clumps. Take strands in each hand and cross them back and forth, pulling tightly. Repeat with every strand until you have a fluff-tastic pom. It takes a long time to fluff your new poms, so plan a get-together to make it more fun.

Your poms need to last the whole year, so follow these tips to avoid wear and tear.

* Poms should only be used when performing, not practicing.
* Keep poms away from heat and water.
* Store poms in a special pom bag when not in use.

Sign Language

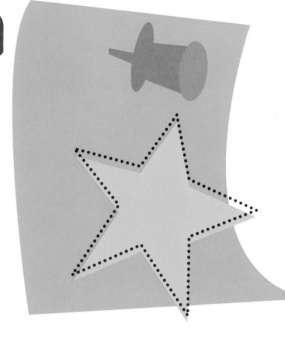

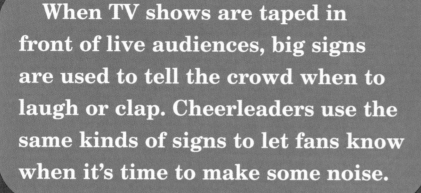

When TV shows are taped in front of live audiences, big signs are used to tell the crowd when to laugh or clap. Cheerleaders use the same kinds of signs to let fans know when it's time to make some noise.

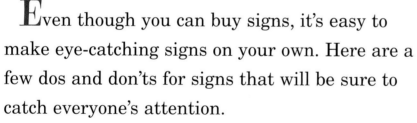

Even though you can buy signs, it's easy to make eye-catching signs on your own. Here are a few dos and don'ts for signs that will be sure to catch everyone's attention.

Do keep it simple. Draw thick letters that are easy to see from afar. Use bold colors that stand out on the sign and outline letters with glitter or black.

Don't put too much on your signs. If your signs are too busy with lots of words and designs, the crowd won't be able to read them.

Don't use thin paper. For sturdy, lasting signs, use strong posterboard.

Do use the power of two. For a twice-as-good effect, one cheerleader can kneel with a sign while another teammate holds the same sign atop a stunt.

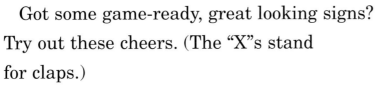

Got some game-ready, great looking signs?
Try out these cheers. (The "X"s stand
for claps.)

*For this cheer, divide the crowd in half and use
signs reading "GREEN" and "WHITE."*

Tigers X
On This Side Yell
Green X GREEN
Tigers X
On This Side Yell
White X WHITE
Put It All Together, Crowd!
GREEN AND WHITE

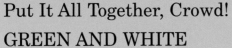

For this cheer, make signs reading "Go Big Blue" and "Beat Those Cats."

Tiger Crowd
Shout It Loud
Yell "Go Big Blue"
GO BIG BLUE
Tiger Crowd
Shout It Loud
Yell "Beat Those Cats"
BEAT THOSE CATS
GO BIG BLUE!
BEAT THOSE CATS!

Try these tips for speaking "sign" language.

This Side Up Draw an arrow on the back so you don't end up holding your signs upside down. Also, they should read from left to right from the crowd's point of view.

Simplicity Rules Limit signs to one letter or word.

On the Level Use level changes to let the crowd know when to respond. For instance, hold the sign at your waist before the crowd's response. Then, lift the sign above your head when it's time for everyone to respond.

"Put it all together!"

Shout It Loud and Proud

Want to get *really* loud? Use a megaphone! The megaphone turns up your voice and looks great on the sidelines. Usually, the captain leads cheers with a megaphone while the squad performs the motions.

The crowd will be looking at your megaphones, so take time to doll them up. Use colored tape, paint, and stickers to make them more eye-catching. Stuck for ideas? Decorate using your name, team logo, or sayings like "Tigers Are #1!"

Cheerleaders shouldn't rely only on megaphones to be heard. It's important to know how to cheer loudly and clearly without one. Here are a few tips on belting it out.

* Don't sing or yell in a high-pitched voice.
* Breathe in deeply to fill lungs with air, and then yell as you breathe out.
* Don't look down while yelling. Keep your gaze on the audience.
* Drink lots of water.
* Yell from your chest, not your throat.

"Use a megaphone!"

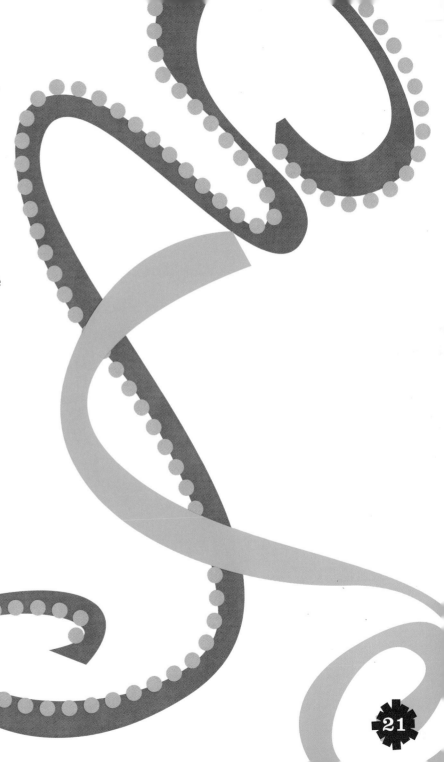

CATCH THE SPIRIT

Mascot Madness

What's fun, furry, and filled with cheer spirit? The team mascot!

A mascot is a "team player," in a sense, who performs with your squad at games and events. Mascots get the crowd excited and add humorous fun to your routines.

" **What's fun, furry, and filled with cheer spirit?** "

Here are some important qualities to look for in a mascot.

* Ability to make up moves on the spot
* Outgoing, silly personality
* School spirit
* Gymnastic or physical ability

Unlike cheerleaders, mascots are dressed in costume, so they don't have to worry about the look on their faces. It's more important that they can move easily in the costume and know how to really play up their movements.

With a mascot on board, you can also include him or her into cheers and funny routines. Most importantly, give the mascot a cute name like "Bobo the Bear." The crowd will love the newest addition to your cheer family.

Put Your Stamp on Cheerleading Camp

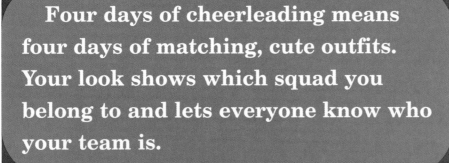

Four days of cheerleading means four days of matching, cute outfits. Your look shows which squad you belong to and lets everyone know who your team is.

When choosing camp clothing, keep in mind that you'll be spending all day cheering (often in the hot sun). It's important to be comfortable. Tank tops and cap-sleeved T-shirts are terrific, while track shorts and cotton skirts are smart bottom choices. Show off with sayings like "Life Is Short. Cheer Hard."

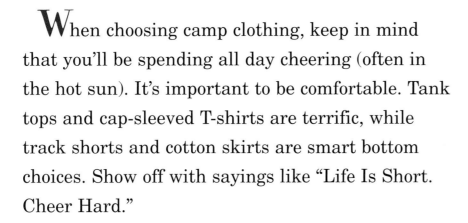

During camp competitions, go for a more polished look by wearing your uniforms. Make the judges take notice with your clean, smart style.

To set yourself apart from other teams, dress on the wild side. Crazy hair bows or face paint are always a big hit, as well as baseball caps and looks that go with a saying. For instance, if your saying is "Tigers Rock!" you can wear a "Tigers" T-shirt and go as wacky as you dare with your hair and makeup.

Playing Dress-Up

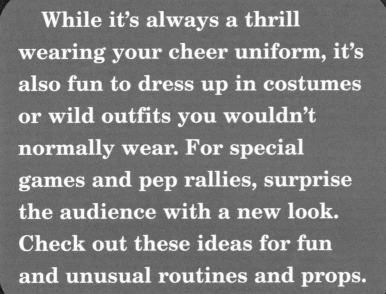

While it's always a thrill wearing your cheer uniform, it's also fun to dress up in costumes or wild outfits you wouldn't normally wear. For special games and pep rallies, surprise the audience with a new look. Check out these ideas for fun and unusual routines and props.

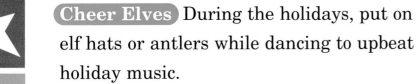 During the holidays, put on elf hats or antlers while dancing to upbeat holiday music.

B-Girls Show off your city moves with a breakdancing routine and wild urban look. Use cardboard boom boxes as props.

Cowgirls Put on your cowboy hats and line up for a line dance! You'll win your way into the audience's "Achy, Breaky Heart."

Role Switch Convince the football players to lend your squad their jerseys for a routine that's sure to score. Start out in a pretend huddle and earn serious points with the crowd.

Although using props is fun and different, remember to practice with your props beforehand so your routine doesn't fall flat.

Winning Fund-raisers

If your team's cash supply is nothing to cheer for, don't worry about it. Fund-raisers are a great way to help fill your squad's piggy bank.

Kiddie Clinic Get ready to teach a group of cheerleaders-in-training! Invite local children to a one-day cheer lesson. They'll love learning simple cheers and dance numbers. Stage a routine for parents at the end of the day.

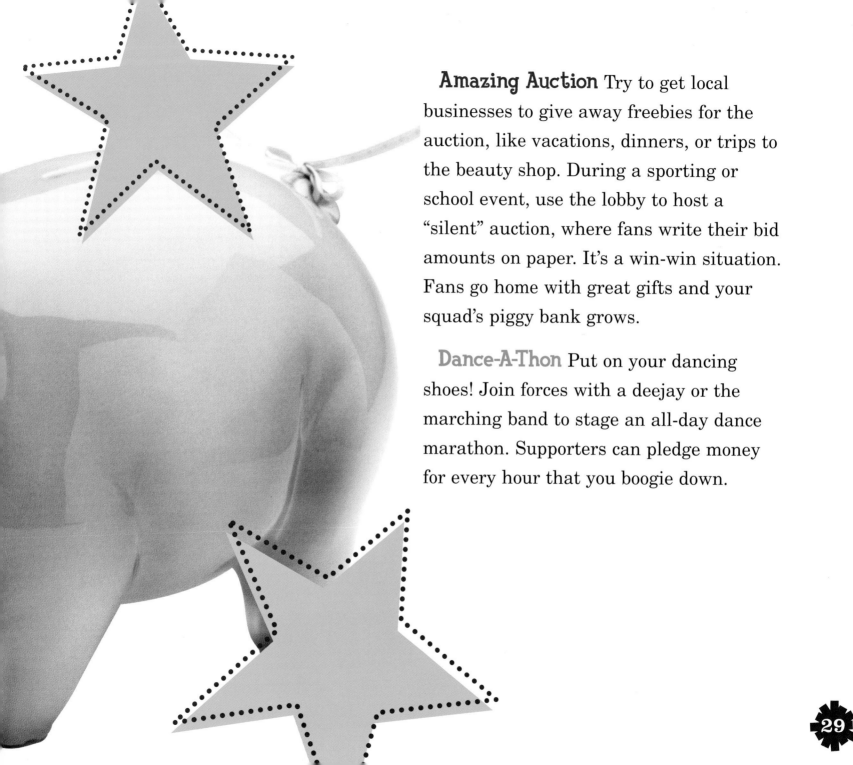

Amazing Auction Try to get local businesses to give away freebies for the auction, like vacations, dinners, or trips to the beauty shop. During a sporting or school event, use the lobby to host a "silent" auction, where fans write their bid amounts on paper. It's a win-win situation. Fans go home with great gifts and your squad's piggy bank grows.

Dance-A-Thon Put on your dancing shoes! Join forces with a deejay or the marching band to stage an all-day dance marathon. Supporters can pledge money for every hour that you boogie down.

GLOSSARY

accessories (ak-SESS-uh-reez) items that make your outfit more interesting, like purses

competition (kom-puh-TISH-uhn) a contest in which two or more people are trying to win the same thing

crosstrainers (KRAWSS-tray-nuhrz) sneakers that can be worn for different sports

essentials (i-SEN-shuhlz) things that you must have for a certain activity

fund-raiser (FUND RAY-zur) an event put on to raise money for a cause

logo (LOH-goh) a symbol or picture that stands for a team or brand

megaphone (MEG-uh-fone) a cone-shaped device used to make your yells louder

routine (roo-TEEN) a set of cheers and chants performed in order, or a dance number to chosen music

shell tops (SHEL TOPS) sleeveless, snug-fitting cheerleader tops

shock absorbent shoes (SHOK ab-ZOR-bent SHOOZ) sneakers for athletic squads

squad (SWKAHD) a team of cheerleaders

strands (STRANDZ) strips of something, such as the vinyl strands of poms

vinyl (VYE-nuhl) a thin type of plastic used to make the strands of poms

FAST FACTS

Here is some must-know info about taking care of your cheerleading uniform.

* Most uniforms should be machine or hand washed in cold water, not dry cleaned.

* Fabric softener makes it harder to get stains out.

* Letting your uniform air-dry after washing it will help prevent wrinkling.

READ MORE

Golden, Suzi J. and Roger Schreiber. *101 Best Cheers: How to Be the Best Cheerleader Ever.* New York: Troll Communications, 2001.

McElroy, James T. *We've Got Spirit: The Life and Times of America's Greatest Cheerleading Team.* New York: Berkley Publishing Group, 2000.

Neil, Randy and Elaine Hart. *The Official Cheerleader's Handbook.* New York: Fireside, 1986.

Peters, Craig. *Competitive Cheerleading.* Broomall, Pennsylvania: Mason Crest, 2003.

Wilson, Leslie. *The Ultimate Guide to Cheerleading.* New York: Three Rivers Press, 2003.

INTERNET SITES

FactHound offers a safe, fun way to find Internet sites related to this book. All of the sites on FactHound have been researched by our staff.

Here's how

1. Visit *www.facthound.com*

2. Type in this special code **0736843604** for age-appropriate sites. Or enter a search word related to this book for a more general search.

3. Click on the **Fetch It** button. FactHound will fetch the best sites for you!

ABOUT THE AUTHOR

While growing up in Ohio, Jen Jones spent seven years as a cheerleader for her grade-school and high-school squads. Following high school, she coached several cheer squads to team victory. For two years, she also cheered and created dance numbers for the Chicago Lawmen semi-professional football dance team.

Jen gets her love of cheerleading honestly, because her mother, sister, and cousins are also heavily involved in the sport. As well as teaching occasional dance and cheerleading workshops, Jen now works in sunny Los Angeles as a freelance writer for publications like *American Cheerleader* and *Dance Spirit*.

Index